THE GUESTS AT THE GATE

The Guests at the Gate

Poems by
ANTHONY PICCIONE

Introduction by
ROBERT BLY

AMERICAN POETS CONTINUUM SERIES, NO. 74

BOA Editions, Ltd. ❦ Rochester, NY ❦ 2002

First Edition
02 03 04 05 7 6 5 4 3 2 1

Publications by BOA Editions, Ltd.—
a not-for-profit corporation under section 501 (c) (3)
of the United States Internal Revenue Code—
are made possible with the assistance of grants from
the Literature Program of the New York State Council on the Arts,
the Literature Program of the National Endowment for the Arts,
the Sonia Raiziss Giop Charitable Foundation,
the Lannan Foundation,
as well as from the Mary S. Mulligan Charitable Trust,
the County of Monroe, NY, Citibank,
Ames-Amzalak Memorial Trust,
and The CIRE Foundation.

See page 72 for special individual acknowledgments.

Cover Design: Daphne Poulin-Stofer
Cover Photograph: Sarah Piccione
Interior Design and Typesetting: Richard Foerster
Manufacturing: McNaughton & Gunn, Lithographers
BOA Logo: Mirko

LIBRARY OF CONGRESS CATALOGING-IN-PUBLICATION DATA

Piccione, Anthony.
  The guests at the gate : poems / by Anthony Piccione ; preface by Robert Bly.
    p. cm. — (American poets continuum series ; no. 74)
  "A paperback original."
  ISBN 1-929918-26-7 (alk. paper)
  1. New York (State)—Poetry. 2. China—Poetry. I. Title. II. Series.

PS3566.I26 G84 2002
811'.54—dc21

                                                        2002024662

BOA Editions, Ltd.
Steven Huff, Publisher
Richard Garth, Chair
A. Poulin, Jr., President & Founder (1976–1996)
260 East Avenue, Rochester, NY 14604
www.boaeditions.org

for the clans
Rizzitano and Piccione
Chandler and Crawford
astonishing exiles and immigrants all

CONTENTS

༜ **In Cool Twilight**

༜ **Looking Up Quickly**

TONY PICCIONE AND THE WOODSTOVE

Tony Piccione belongs to a tribe of people who are easily wounded, who clamber along in the raccoon darkness, who never entirely get over it if you shout at them. I never did shout at Tony, so what would I know about it? But I did feel him rumbling through the dark, as passionate for truth as a baby bear for honey. He is never really at home in the tops of trees or at academic parties.

> The cabin silent again, the woodstove gathers speed,
> and there is no work to be done. I say to them,
> my brain-lodged selves, I love this unwavering place,
> my days and my death so near and so openly mine.

He goes along, with God not far away. It seems to him the dead are all around him; it is some dense cloudiness they carry around them, like a willowy swamp, like the sound of flutes in Bali that accompany the mourners, like the dimness one senses at nightfall in the forest, that darkness close to the ground. His eyes are gleaming; he is not complaining about what he doesn't receive; he is a lively companion of what will happen next.

> How easy, to awake into the powering world
> and turn at once to God, the orphaned saint,
> the madman wrestling through, or to it,
> my own thick-shanked homespun life
> grinning into the face of what may happen next.
> This is my time, my footstep, my stalled
> and sprongy witness on earth.

So it's like the route, where there are always checkpoints. Everyone has to know what we are doing. When you are twenty-five, it's the brain that becomes heated over what may come and what may stop; but now it's the lower body that knows what is going on, the stomach oven that registers what is ahead on the forest path. "One birth, one death," someone cries out, "Place your bets!" So we each have a house in which we were born, then we are impelled by hope and fear into a new house, and then comes the third, the saving presence, which is neither in our parents' home, nor in the absence from our parents' home, but it is a solid place, right here, with our wife, our gladness, our work, our desire.

> How we gain and fail at every checkpoint
> and all the while the belly flames with hope and fear.
> One birth then, one death, so says the companion
> of the first day. One home, one hurtling exile,
> and one reckoning only, arisen, in the center,
> in my shoes, shaped by all I yet desire.

This collection of poems gradually builds until it reaches in the last four or five poems a "mind of place arisen and complete."

> Go well, oh anyone awake and marveling,
> pray hard for what you are about to receive.

Let's do one more poem without any good-willed interruptions this time. I have done some interruptions so that the poem will pass more slowly the spot where we are standing, but this poem goes as it goes.

> I walk on out into the blur of things
> until my heart surrounds a faint belonging.
> What attends at birth has turned from us,
> I am guessing, or waits nearby
> for a kind of return. I don't know. Is it true,
> neighbor? I have heard your cries.
>
> Uneasy in this, sent out from myself,
> what drops away and rises just ahead
> is a lonely joy winding back to the sea.
> But I'd root down if I could, if there were time,
> learn the ways, joke with those who abide.
> There's a pale hand over me pushes me along.
>
> I keep staggering about, wrong name, wrong face.
> I'd like to stay for once inside a town,

to fix cars or want to, or work for the railroad,
deliver the mail, consult seriously with others.
I want to come in, start over, forget altogether
that the star giver breathes in us, that we stumble on.

In the last line, we hear words that James Wright might have written, and that is good. Wright was a mentor of Tony's, from a long distance, as is proper. Toward the end of his life, Wright would not allow anyone to depress him or to say that all this misery is confused. It is going somewhere! We all stumble on, but so does the star giver.

How easily we take life to ourselves, what we
wished for, even the trouble, love, children, calling, all
of it pulling us to our knees in feverish good play. It is
a great gift, that kneeling, no matter what we've done.

We have to say goodbye now to this sweet man, worthy of his family, his struggles and his language! Farewell!

—Robert Bly

Dear Friend

NOTE BITS

July 3, 1999

How strange at the end of a day at the last of our century that we can still remember how to survive each other at all. How we keep the front door tells it, the massive wood or steel slab between us and the relentless force of machine and speed we've given over to, just to belong to a world. We know by the way our lives tremble and divide. Once inside, though, the hum of electrical charge trailing off along our fingers, there is a quiet which blesses and washes us clean of what governs or scorns our human slowness, our joy and our play. We know what *door* means by what the belly feels. The phone bleats, the glassine envelopes quiver on the table, the t.v. yawns itself to death, the newspapers open, something keeps thumbing the buzzer, pawing the doorknob.

BECAUSE I LISTENED

In bed at nine I'd drift along unsleeping
and track the grown-ups in their kitchen talk,
measuring the silences, the sudden shifts of spirit.
I felt the odd buzzing in my ear was God
somehow, a flutter like a doorbell under water.
So I wept and waited, sensing a far off time,
the voices fumbling on, the day begun to fold upon itself.

I wanted to ask for more but swallowed the words instead.
Fifty years have called me on. And it's *tinnitus,*
but I know what it is. These days I lie down
into the *ohhh* a ship makes at full ahead
as the engines stop. I'll listen hard.
There is a stillness to the slowing rush. Now
a boy wakes, stares, sets out to fulfill a world.

TRADING PLACES IN A POEM

Let's say you are you and nobody else.
I just appear, walking in the neuron fields
along your twilit starry brain. I bring news
and our fear of heights. Now you are *you*
meaning me and a few others leaning over the page.
So what. We greet each other roughly and agree
it's a tender, lonely place to put a homeland.
It pulls at us that we still add up to one, *one*,
and there's the wary chafe between self and stranger.
We open our hands to vastness beyond edge,
to worlds without end. And the doors tremble
open, crowds in all directions, our shoulders touch,
the quick jazz of energy, now six billion dancers
on an eyelash, yours, neighbor, spun from gold.

TOWN MEETING

I show up early and sit in the back. Something's jumpy
in me, from childhood, aching and alone, but I find myself
standing with the others. The old pledge to the flag
is still whole in me, safe among the keepers of words,
the heroes so carefully tucked.

These faces are enduring, open, unbeaten,
the white-haired stubble says so when they speak,
and the women in their solid, hopeful power speak.
There is a solitary rightness in what they ask.

I left and lost this country half a century ago,
felt it fade and vanish into a dot of time
over my shoulder, *my* time I went out from and wept for
into the world seeking a life. And it is here,
in a handful of unrelenting survivors, without guile,
or scheme, or the desire to live forever.

EARLY MORNING FAREWELL
TO BERNIE SCHUSTER

Slumped at the table, alive to the words of one who survived
until yesterday, what can I offer except to weep into my hands?
But a sudden music pushes out through the radio, a surprise
rises in the chest, a sweeping half-memory of Persia, or Syria,
Jerusalem maybe, the strong softness of women in dance,
the wisp of wind, the evening hushing down its moist whisper.

What have I been welcomed into so easily? That time
goes on furling around our feet in delicate surround? That
what has left us keeps arriving, returned, just out of reach?
I'll taste this delight, I think, for my friend so still in body,
so majestically now a part of the breeze, dust, air, figs, shouts,
so much the shiver of breath, shoulder, veil, so nearly always near.

DOWN IN PRATTSBURGH, NEW YORK

We go out our doors into the shove of people
and it is made of scorn and cloud and a bit of hope.
Sometimes, suddenly alive, happy about a small thing,
our snares withdraw, day blazes higher,
a deep good light scours the walks and storefronts.
The tiny bells over the shop doors sing softly *here, here,*
for we, insanely at home, step into ourselves and begin to speak.

TALKING LATE AT NIGHT

Sprawled awake, dumb with my wife after love,
I am surprised to hold a secret and think of telling her
I sink with the senses so full so far out ahead
into a pool spilling with canned peaches,
the smooth shivery viscous kiss of her
now in the mouth of touch on all sides.

I'm slow to speak. I know something's off
in me to think at all, but the face inside the face,
so anciently lost and returned at the edge
as we turn our heads to see.

What of it if we swoon delirious
by loving, by feeling our way along
the simple tracks and leaf stems, the configurations
and feathers and hieroglyphs crisscrossing the world,
the sugary brain of fruit so absolutely wet and sweet?

The body rocks us forward more surely each day.
Bending over a shoe, picking up a spoon, we are here
at last to be born, alive, in the self to be given.

DEAR FRIEND

Sat down to read your book in one sitting and would have, only I kept lifting my head to return, to test my heart on the woods just beyond and once again on the words.

The world is true all right, and it is so that I eased dreamily sideways through three wars without trying, pulled along by my own rasping aloneness, in God-craving exile, flailed, grief-sweetened, and the dull whine of governments the real fiction, ghosts crackling over the slopes just out of sight.

So many lives on Earth, life itself the oddity, and I raised up a few times, and looked down. What, except for unwavering grief, has it to do with me? Everything, which at this black curve in time is not enough, not even nearly.

We have love, sorrow, rage, what we hope will happen next, and they are voices praying out loud as before a great waterfall.

God bless you. God bless your words.

Gathering the News

STEPPING ACROSS

Our feet sensed the shuddering will of it and then the great silent heave beneath at impossible angle, the final edge of our century tilting madly, about to go down. We've felt certain that time does not move or remotely resemble a deck buckling, but we also know that ideas do, inside our dream of time-span and space, and this was our raft of one hundred years.

What a century to wake to. Steam to atom, horsehoof to rocket, wires of the voice-tongue and ear to everywhere, Tibet, undersea, moon, the body peeling away to reveal a trace spark, the soul not there, but everywhere at once. In play, hamburger of thing, gadget, tool, toy, shovelful of the sun itself squeezed down into bomb shapes cold to the touch, war-kissed, love-held, gender-mind flown round with comets, children risen from the brain of secrets, Creation nearly near but spilling through our hands once more, and we love that the crazy last, least one shall be first, that miracle of quirky divine, after all. People raising the great cathedral, the poor come in, the laugh of play and shove of forgive, in absolute uncertainty, the small light alive over the doom of minds at the end and even that was temporary, and eternal.

STEPHEN HAWKING AND FELLINI

1

Out from the archway, the shadows seeming a wall, he is gliding softly towards us in that small three-wheeled scooter chair, his poor great head nodding with the bumps over the brick passageway, his smile fixed and somehow real, his mind aloft in electronic voice. He is calm about the few threads trailing beautifully out from Genesis into our century. He's gone far, we sense, but who could endure that dimming distant edge? We see he can still move one finger a little, or almost, on the telepathic control box darkening beneath his hand. He speaks in a sing-song lilt of electrical sparks.

in our beginning   one upheaval
our rewinding   one stupendous dot

2

Into the grainy graying Italian street comes Zampano the Amazing, he can shatter chains with his massive chest, one great insucking of breath is all. Sweet Gelsomina is shy to trumpet his showy masculine arrival. What they have is the little tent house on the back of his rickety tri-motor-cycle. His unyielding face, his pride of strength and the infinity of the opening road have cost him his soul, we are guessing. He is the one we pity for aloneness in doom, even as we ache for Gelsomina, the birdlike daughter cast adrift in childhood . . .

3

Out of time, the one who would read God's sugary mind leans forward, or seems to think of leaning forward, making the mewing whispers of a man too exhausted, or whose tongue has been pulled out, one who knows too much and now must speak without parting his lips. Now his assistant bends near, agreeing, and begins incredibly to translate.

out along the cobble path
in burning speed of stars

though we plunge on
what impossible joy

stitching restitching
so dazzlingly spun

the way open empty
to be a human being

FOR THE ONE TO COME

The infant's delicate forehead a beacon of promise,
his perfect human face, all that we are
depends on him, his stare from the other world,
his great, unblinking eyes so new to earth.

The miraculous one keeps rising among us.
Now do we turn, and rush to prepare the way.

HIS FACE

Shadowy police shapes crowd over a man kneeling and crawling at their feet, two or three of them taking turns at the black sticks which lift and fall upon him, but he will not lie still. He keeps making as though to rise, to take the blows on his arms, so they flail on. Whatever he has done beyond the twilight reach of the camera, I am for him, but weakly, and turn away.

It is clear what century this is, what drives the night sticks into a man so busily. Eyes smeared shut with their own bone and ooze, mouth ruined, hands frozen in agony, this is slowly gathering in me, no riddling of words can shift the nightmare to news event. A stranger has been surrounded by law and beaten into puffy surrender. His face looks over in radiant pain. Maybe we ought to raise our hands to take the next few strikes. They say he knelt, would not stop kneeling, and the face, so softly ashamed, lingers in the air around, like love, or dread, or holy failure.

LOCAL WRITER

It's a good stubbly face, tightening with pain.
He's sprawled over the chair, older than I am,
and seems always to know things oddly,
from the back woods farm he grew up on,
down quarry country, he tells me.
He turns away, blowing his nose.

Anything leaves tracks leaves a story,
he says sideways, opening the handkerchief.
See? Woodstove needs cleaned soon.
Cigarettes'll kill you long before you quit,
and there's way too much dust on those beams.

Jabbing at the bright flecks and fibers
spread out in his hand like alphabets,
he looks at me, suddenly grinning.
Imagination is just a remembering,
from the other side, of course.

BOW SEASON

I've watched their muddy jeep inch
along the half mile drive to my barn
where I pretend to be busy, and look up
at the last second. The younger one
springs out and walks over, he's wary,
he's heard about me.

The boy wants to know if he can cull
a deer or two out of the small herd
that seems to remember, each autumn,
there is a dark deepening to these woods.
Nothing gets killed or *culled* on this land,
I hear myself, the words are cold and stiffly apart.
I follow his eyes, suddenly hating him somehow,
that sickly other, skinny, shifting, raising up
and come for us at last. Whatever it is

that hums below our human strangeness
is awake in me, older, beyond brain or belonging.
Now he backs off, careful to look down, for
he sees it too, I sense, the matted creatures
closing in, the wild hairy one fiercely stunned.
We measure each other, half turning away.
In a while, I know, the words will begin
winging down, what I may say to ease a neighbor,
but I am like a man running downhill,
backwards, awkward, ugly, towards what is mine.

WATCHING THE EVENING NEWS

A river of them, olive bronze men in glistening fatigues,
the long columns high stepping double time in awkward procession,
shiny black rifles tight to the chest, eyes right in a vacant fix—
it's as though they've studied the war films of grainy nightmare
and chosen the dark apprentice again, for a certain style, a quickness
and leave to crush past and future, parents and children, the old,
    the weak,
and so to show up rested, eager, hurtling into the next unleashing,
    a school,
a few towns, a mountainside of watchful monks, whatever aches to
    endure.

There's a sudden sweeping sickness in me, not for the upswing of
    horror,
not simply that, but for the unshameable one so close to home.
He is like an uncle broken loose again, shackles clinking at the wrists,
storefronts in flames, the dead and dying behind him. His happiness
    so public,
so doomed, he stands saluting the wind, untouched by all we've
    lived to know.
I want to look away. I want to take up my grief, gather with others,
    go on.

ENTERING GENESEE GORGE

The tangling weave of leaf and branch releases.
We awake suddenly and at last upon a great
bristling stillness, an urge to kneel and rise
at once, as inside the chest of a cathedral.

Through the muscular rock and starkly
forested upheave a river goes on arriving.
Now the soundless clench over ears
gives way to the roaring spill of waterfall.

The sky is also new, or it was always here,
strangely alive. A massive billowing cloudbank
weighs down upon all that surrounds until witness
itself enters the dark, powering, luminous presence.

Oddly heroic, then, is the squat waterwheel shack
hunched alone in its task to part the tumbling rush
and to creak on in its cogs to the grinding of bread.
Stiff, rickety, a footbridge spans the gorge and holds.

Incredibly, two robed figures, women, or monks, or angelic
visitors from another time—are walking across. Their words,
so invisible and tiny, go forth to whisper into nations.
Above them, feathery beings pause, lift upon the updraft.

—on the painting "Genesee Scenery" by Thomas Cole

SITTING IN THE MALL WHILE MY WIFE DOES ALL THE WORK

She settles me in like a child at the little island of benches
and goes off, hopeful and waving as I join the others,
mostly slouching men who stare lazily above me
as though at a wall out past the last row of audience.
I imagine we're all Cancerians watching from a private place.
You can spot us sometimes slowing in a crowd, though slumping,
strength flying out into people as in a snowstorm in reverse.

There's something too public about this group, its sulking pose.
We're the entire team sent back to the minor leagues
and now we refuse to move. We size each other sideways
with that impatient blowout of breath. One looks from his watch
into the workmanship of the ceiling. The stage reveals us
to ourselves! Condemned, exempt, though we've little more to hide,
we sit tongueless, like immigrants lost in a courtyard of Babel.

What's down below but all of time? But what flits around inside?
There's the hammock man napping while others toil, that's easy.
And just as God in the brain gives up in disgust, the crowd
turns to squint at the fugitive caught in the spotlight.
We have seed-dreaming man. No woman, tree or blade of grass
is free of his clumsy lunge to spawn the oceans and the earth.
What else seethes in shackles? Liar. Grabber. Feasting king.

How odd, to lounge alone in this coolly distant realm,
because my enemies despise me from a darkened room.
Not snarlers only, but the faithful guides stand blinking,
pauper, hermit, receiver of praise, even the child in chains.
Confessor, pilgrim, bridge for the feet of duty,
how pale we've all become. And who cut us apart, and when?
A skulking power squeezes the heart and calls the bosses in.

Now and again a man stands and shuffles off.
The shadowy light that has held his face flickers out,
a tightness takes over, his years of age suddenly return.
But what to make of the hidden country, the brightly dully doomed?
We've dodged or endured the blasts of murderers and saints, and now
these walls are folding. Nothing holds forever. We sense the news.
So many twisting guests to be kissed at the gate, and led inside.

What Calls Out for Us

NEIGHBORS AND EXILES

Sometimes a power enters and heaves around for a name, like *vortex*, a darkness of anti-matter surrounding the odd, brief spark of good intention. A faint, crackly implosion stuns us when the language is twisted to lie, and the world moves off and stands apart.

Strange that we've kept watch against lying at all, it moves so easily through us, hauling our phantoms and embalmings behind, and gives off the reek of hospital waiting rooms. We have to think hard to figure the times we join this creature, though it oozes so easily near. We're just its neighbor, we say, surprised to see the trail circle back to our feet when we look down. When we come upon them, people wounded by a flick of the tongue, our sentences rush to begin with *but*.

But everything weakens, the world plunges on,
the bright white bursts of words freezing behind us
as we go. In these days of dizzying exile, forgiveness
aches like a seedrow sutured into the brain, its
syllable buds lifting with our hope and our pain.

READING ALL NIGHT AT THE TABLE

Little winged creatures,
about the size of commas,
quaint infinitesimal flying dogs
dizzied by the blinding white between words
on the page I am reading—seem somehow
to trust me. I've grown strangely fond, it's true,
and now I have to ferry them out on a matchbook cover
before turning the page. They seem always at home in their play,
circling, waiting, hurrying me to catch up, to move on.

WITH MY WIFE IN LATE NOVEMBER

We arise early, tired, slow minded,
and ponder awhile the odd
iridescence of the lowering cloud dome.
Only a few jobs to do this morning,
we get to joking, our hands touch lightly.

We make the north rise through the drifts
and bolt a good chain across the old gate path
for nothing more than we abide now with
the solitary ones, the rabbits, voles, the grazers
under the crust, the feathery watchers around,
and ache to keep the snowmobilers off, just for once,
our restless townsmen chasing down the cold, unreachable speed
out past a ragged, snarly, deafening blast at stillness.

I think these things. I know something close is lost
against the rush of people, some of them, anyway,
but I stand there, kinship stiffening in my chest,
my fist cursing the air, the other, *that* one.

AT BREAKFAST

1

I sit slouched at the table, marveling,
the earth so close when there are daughters.
But the son has also grown wild in a body
packed with sparks of power. Then it is 1945,
I am alive, gap-toothed, giddy,
plunging about in wide amazement.

2

Out into the sweet summery fog,
love of play calls us to extinction
and through it, to a shore of the other side.

Sometimes a guardian presence around children
arrives, a kind of shape in shadow,
for they are still only almost in the world.

3

If there is a razor blade too sharp to touch,
if there is a pulsing fingertip, and a boy
grappling with *sharp* or *too* or *touch*, come down.

And if a tanker car waits in the weed-blown siding,
and a match-flame sputters above the watery fumes,
come near. If a black bull stares from a field.

Where there is a cottonmouth unfolding on the path,
or one rifle shell gleaming darkly on the table,
the boy's hammer poised and trembling, come to us now.

SOMETHING FEEDING ON NIGHT

Whatever it is sipping at our marrow
flits back into a face so sweetly close
in the light that it may be only a dream.
But then all day the heart sags and aches
for word, sifting clues or blurring signs,
the taste of omen souring out in open air.

Maybe a wife goes mad in the wake of a life
undelivered. We think yes. What has attended
that child through the inconsolable hours
stacks a slow, untouchable fortune: everything.
And steps inside her bones to outwait death.
She, silent watcher at our weddings, births,
passages, this one will not move or blink.

What we do as right can barely lift us, or else
there is a light-devouring other in every breast,
so patiently at hand when the self weakens and lets go,
as, so sudden in the flick of exchange, the face
we almost know, familiar, as oddly kindred as skin
or scar over the sky-pounded world, snaps awake.

STARTLED AT THE TOUCH
OF OTHERNESS

The sugary outpourings of the human tongue
all true, not enough true, if we begin and end.

Where my groping ascension needs its consent,
it must also attend my unremarkable collapses.

Where are we off to, then? The heights foretell
our lowing rootedness, the heart rejoices in its meaty self,

the world of all else unfolds its slow and holy insistence.

JUST AS SOMETHING CALLS

(for Leslie)

I lie down in a field between two pine groves
and lift my head, listening. Far off, near Cleveland,
I feel my sister weaving and reweaving her prayer shawl.
The tiny herds of cancer in her bones stand ice-still.

North of here, bound from Canada, our Yankton healer
rests waiting in a thicket for the patrol to pass.
Their radio yowls as they dip over the rise into silence.
His snowshoes whisper as he takes up his bag and moves on.

There are medicine herbs that glow when people are near, and
now we are a part of his sky. For this he labors across borders
in the deepening cold, the miles close behind him like sea waves,
his agony anoints our lives and calls us out, and we come.

SENSE OF SOMETHING ABOUT TO HAPPEN

A stillness rounds the air out over the treeline, my kingdom,
and the mind-sized yard keeps glowing like a tomb of light.

If then a woman suddenly arrived with her bags of things
in both arms, the world might move again towards kindness.

Anyone, stepped up onto the porch, would be a delight,
oh, easy benediction, and the day could go on falling.

Such aloneness, at last, is a sky over our grief,
the afternoon slowing, looking up, listening hard.

In Cool Twilight

WINTER 1992.   MARCH.

1

There's usually enough light to read by, and at night we turn the lamps on, set way down to a flicker. The wind stopped all day on the 12th. There's enough wood to last all of April, probably.

Can't blame it, they're saying. The weather's different, all right, and that's no joke this once. You never see a spring like this one, but you might, somebody said.

We left the pick-up down by the road, and had to shovel it out twice just to get it there. The drifts are deep. When my wife leaves for work I watch until she gets to the curve and stops to rest and wave back. The way she chooses a path, thinking about each step, looks like a deer from so far away.

2

I have the feeling sometimes that things are turning backwards to their time. Where I'm standing feels like the ground is sinking. The year I was ten, I'd float back through the Romans, Greeks, Egyptians, the stilt settlements, to where the books stopped. I kept picturing a place by a fire in the Ice Age, there wasn't much history for it, except it was hard, it didn't help you, you were on your own, and even if everybody died, the ice had its own life to stiffen and grow towards, going its way to where the world rests and has no further need.

I RISE EARLY, AND STUMBLE ON

The hidden one must be exhausted, slumped
inside my ribcage, unheeded, unsummoned.
I need a teaspoon, it flies
under the stove, so carefully do I reach for it.
I rub my eyes, unthankful and half-amazed.
Coffee beans leap from my hand like confetti bits.
Somewhere my lost sock endures a life alone.
Comedy and doom. On these days I am the thief
who waits too long. A tiny steamshovel inches the prize
over, drops it just short, so close, too bad.
What am I then, so slow in this playful body,
clumsy, unholy, lurching towards a thought?
Where there is no honoring, there is no man.
A voice says this, far off, in our brain.

RISING PAST DAWN

It's early, our two dogs crash about in the cold,
a sideways sleet drives the light into the snowbanks.
The cabin silent again, the woodstove gathers speed,
and there is no work to be done. I say to them,
my brain-lodged selves, I love this unwavering place,
my days and my death so near and so openly mine.

How easy, to awake into the powering world
and turn at once to God, the orphaned saint,
the madman wrestling through, or to *it*,
my own thick-shanked homespun life
grinning into the face of what may happen next.
This is my time, my footstep, my stalled
and sprongy witness on earth.

How we gain and fail at every checkpoint
and all the while the belly flames with hope and fear.
One birth then, one death, so says the companion
of the first day. One home, one hurtling exile,
and one reckoning only, arisen, in the center,
in my shoes, shaped by all I yet desire.

OUT INTO TWILIGHT, EARLY DECEMBER

A few stars, and suddenly thousands poke through,
their pale blue stares cool and weightless on my face.
What luck! to be alive, walking our frozen outpost,
toes numb, trees stark and wildly poised,
the soft spill of light folding on, on, into the world.

NIGHT TRAIN
THROUGH INNER MONGOLIA

Now the child is a runny-nosed stranger
you've finally decided to share your seat with,
and the whole thing keeps heaving into the dark.

The child sleeps unsweetly hunched against you,
your side is slowly stinging, he has wet himself,
so you do not move at all. I know you.

You sit awake, baffling about a quirky faith,
and do not shift until morning. This is why
you are blessed, I think, and usually chosen.

GOING OUTSIDE AS THOUGH I SUDDENLY THOUGHT OF SOMETHING

I take up my stick and start down the good country road,
no cars, centuries of trees leaning in overhead. Each thing
looks like our lives, and everywhere.

Walking, I begin unwinding fifty years of my own sorrow
back down in time to the faces of our ghostly sickened young.
At last those dancers on the dance floor look up, about to touch.

The empty rooms are filling again. The music softens,
rewarming the bones of outcast, our mawkish ennui,
our pallid turn of heart. We welcome ourselves in,

and cover the eyes of television, where we've sent our dead.
Somehow, in these late days, the world still endures our hands,
like words in moonlight, like rounded lifting loaves of bread.

Nearing home, I grow very tired and lie down on the grass.
How delicious, to love a life nearly too long to remember!
This is only my way, I am guessing, and walk on into myself.

LYING DOWN UNDER A TREE AT DUSK

Evening comes hauling and heaving around me,
what I have loved all day gone over to black invisible.
The quick chittering creatures pull up in silence, holding.
Others, fierce presences of rock, bone, sand glint, glow darkly on,
the delicately woven mind of place arisen and complete.

Go well, oh anyone awake and marveling,
pray hard for what you are about to receive.

IN COOL TWILIGHT

I walk on out into the blur of things
until my heart surrounds a faint belonging.
What attends at birth has turned from us,
I am guessing, or waits nearby
for a kind of return. I don't know. Is it true,
neighbor? I have heard your cries.

Uneasy in this, sent out from myself,
what drops away and rises just ahead
is a lonely joy winding back to the sea.
But I'd root down if I could, if there were time,
learn the ways, joke with those who abide.
There's a pale hand over me pushes me along.

I keep staggering about, wrong name, wrong face.
I'd like to stay for once inside a town,
to fix cars or want to, or work for the railroad,
deliver the mail, consult seriously with others.
I want to come in, start over, forget altogether
that the star giver breathes in us, that we stumble on.

Looking Up Quickly

IT'S MORNING

so I lean out of the small upstairs window of the cabin for the breeze passing through our woods. The feather and birdcall air is busy, a kind of weather, and I lean my face into its peppery sting. All the years and I still can't learn the names, so many heaving hurrying ferocities weaving a home in the brain. Mudsucker is woodcock, though. I lean back in.

How easily we take life to ourselves, what we wished for, even the trouble, love, children, calling, all of it pulling us to our knees in feverish good play. It is a great gift, that kneeling, no matter what we've done.

STANDING STILL IN THE POLE BARN

Have we come this far so alone in ourselves?
For night, we can lie down and drift starward,
for what calls is without trace or nameable sign.
How strange to ache and wrestle through time
starving for home.

                I come to, staggered
against the red plow tractor that won't stay fixed,
wild in myself. My knuckles are bloodied.
Beaten again and grinning, I call out to our fathers
and take up the greasy wrench. Its heaviness

is a cold stone in my hand. I lay it on the repair book
boiling with fine Egyptian drawings. I lean down,
the measure of *here, now*, up close to my face,
and chomp on the sweet wet chill of my cigar stub.
What I love is gone before me, lifting the twelve directions.

LOUNGING AWHILE AND KEEPING STILL

We can be standing wrapped around with tangle,
the world and us in it frozen, until something moves
and the heart of it all is changed a little, close or far.

One day a cello might fill the air out to what is barely seen.
There is its grave joy crackling into the silence of telepathy
we can follow, past even the electrical minds of cells and stones,

so that, aching on tiptoe, we step across the edge
of ourselves. And our whole life awaits us there,
so that now, invisible, we can set wildly about to begin.

WATCHING TWO PEOPLE

An old man feeds a feeble woman a slice of cake,
one small bite, then another. Her hands shake terribly
with delight. Their bond is complete. They sustain.
Sometimes, when I finally glimpse a thing come true,
the world strains and falls and we are all massively older.
This thought hurtles like a cannonball into a catcher's mitt,
the entire homeplate section and I fly backwards a mile or two
into the side of a hill where it is forgotten, as we get back up.
He feeds her because what they love they shall receive,
because we rise so lazily, and time suddenly arrives.

AT MY MOTHER'S GRAVE

I know I have stood apart in witness of myself
talking low over a grave, so not to weigh
upon the dead, I don't know why even as I think it.
I guessed for my children once our bodies are doorways
we go dreaming through, out to somewhere near
that grows slowly far. I speak to her now in this way,
mother of departure, she who ached for life so fiercely.

I talk quietly on, she in stillness listens
and they, neighbors and kin and the faces dimming
back to 1741, lie still. The echo faints into my forehead
so I stand stiff as after a lightning strike.
The air is dry and wilting. Fat grasshoppers shake the weeds.
That stone angel trembling on a pillar above my childhood
watches from eye level now. I look across into its blind gaze.

I miss her everywhere. Nearness is more terrible
than death. When I weep, my hands go out alone,
I am cleaning my mother's place. This is her place!
I am still kneeling when dark stoops down.

I have labored in unwavering heat all afternoon.
Nothing is left to me except to make neat, call out
the unsaid days, and lie down on the grass, the mother
I almost know like a question stitching and healing my side.

WHEN LOVE MOVES US

There is our delicate union,
the sweet ache surrounded by longing,
so being blessed is easy, staying whole is hard.

And, being human, we know about exile and belonging.
The way is suddenly clear. We'll need heart, hands, feet,
and the sacrament of *whatever-happens-next!*

CLIMBING DOWN FROM OUR CENTURY

There is the morning when, rising early, the newlywed
steps out of glory and onto the trading floor.
It is already colder in the room, and the need
to lay down a life for another recoils in empty air.
Now the gifts between them shrink back into gestures.

A blunt echo offers that the heart keeps failing us
or somehow blocks a darker realm from view.
The truth is, the Garden itself expels us, so quietly,
in the half-moment before we suddenly decide to plan,
or bulldoze, or outguess our own deer-trail shimmering way.

But we are born upon nothing at all, fingernails bloodied,
slammed against a high ledge, slung a toehold or two
above extinction. But we can reach for each other,
and see into a face, and so love the outstretched world—
it is that delicate and weak, and crazily far from home.

IN THE BODY MADE OF WOMAN

Where breasts are simply and completely true,
to be kissed in amazement, or prayed for,
and desire goes humming happily lost,

we love the voice inside the voice that calls us on,
in pitch and tone and intent so perfectly shrouded,
where, brightly spinning upon its own journey,

within the dark, massive notes down from stars,
something sweet, shifting, never resting in one place,
from this we have paused to make a world.

LOOKING UP QUICKLY

This is a note to soft lipped Mother
whose back I keep glimpsing
as I look up from hauling rocks,
or turn a corner, or lie down defeated,
or come out from the woods for home.

Hearing a woman laugh out loud
without fear or shyness or intention
I suddenly remember
there is the work of a universe.

I gaze into her faces
one goes out to mangoes
one lies down to weep
one watches from between worlds
one builds a wall of stones
one keeps the first fire
one wraps us in swaddling.

ACKNOWLEDGMENTS

Bright Hills Press Anthology: "Town Meeting";
Brown Dog Press: "Watching Two People";
The Coffee House: "His Face," "In Cold Clear Twilight," "Local
    Writer," "Neighbors and Exiles," "Standing Still in the Pole
    Barn," "Trading Places in a Poem";
The English Record: "I Rise Early and Stumble On," "In Cold Clear
    Twilight," "Watching the News";
Exit-Online: "Down in Prattsburgh, New York," "Early Morning
    Farewell to Bernie Schuster," "Sense of Something About to
    Happen," "Talking Late at night";
Lake Affect: "Night Train Through Inner Mongolia";
Prayers For a Thousand Years, "For the One to Come".
Voices in the Gallery, Memorial Art Gallery, Grant Holcomb, editor:
    "Entering Genesee Gorge";

Deep thanks to Zina Pastorelli, Sandi Henschel, and Ginny Lance,
sweet traveling companions.

Ongoing dumbfounded thanks for helping me live and relive the
poems: Li Young, Judi, Robert, Lucien, Barry, Tim, Sandra, Larry,
Carol, Maril, Bill, Ellen, Duane, Miss Jane, Lisa, J. Antonio, Samuel
Antonio, Todd, Rachel, Michael, Sarah, Anthony Joseph.

ABOUT THE AUTHOR

Born in Sheffield, Alabama, and raised in Selden, Long Island, Anthony Piccione was the author of four collections of poetry from BOA Editions, Ltd.: *The Guests at the Gate (2002), For the Kingdom* (1995), *Seeing It Was So* (1986) and *Anchor Dragging* (1978, chosen by Archibald MacLeish for BOA's A. Poulin, Jr. New Poets of America Series). As Professor Emeritus of English and creative writing at the State University of New York College at Brockport, Piccione taught at Upright Hall, the Writers' Retreat at his Crow Hill Farm in Prattsburgh, New York. His poems, interviews, essays and reviews have appeared in dozens of magazines and journals. Anthony Piccione died in November 2001.

SUDDEN RAIN ON MT. JIAN MEN

Coat wine-stained, stiff with dust,
for the traveler, every direction is fantastic!

How, so luckily alive, go on with poetry, astride
a donkey, halfway up the mountain, in light drizzle?

—**Lu You**—
(Tr. 1990, with help
from Carol Chang)

BOA EDITIONS, LTD.

AMERICAN POETS CONTINUUM SERIES

COLOPHON

The Guests at the Gate, Poems by Anthony Piccione,
with a Introduction by Robert Bly,
was set in Galliard, with Monotype Rococo ornaments,
by Richard Foerster, York Beach Maine.
The cover was designed by Daphne Poulin-Stofer,
with a photograph by Sarah Piccione.
Manufacturing was by McNaughton & Gunn,
Saline, Michigan.

Publication of this book was made possible, in part, by the
special support of the following people:
Debra Audet
Laure-Anne Bosselaar & Kurt Brown
Carol Cooper & Howard Haims
Susan De Witt Davie
Pat Ford
Dr. Henry & Beverly French
Dane & Judy Gordon
Kip & Deb Hale
Peter & Robin Hursh
Robert & Willy Hursh
Dorothy & Henry Hwang
Meg Kearney
Archie & Pat Kutz
Robert & Francie Marx
Phil Memmer
Boo Poulin
Deborah Ronnen
David Ryon
Jane Schuster
Robert B. Shea
Allen & Suzy Spencer
Thomas R. Ward
Michael Waters & Mihaela Moscaliuc
Pat & Michael Wilder